A Beautiful Life

A Beautiful Life

A weekly journal to help you
find joy in the every day

Blue Water Books

Richland, Wa

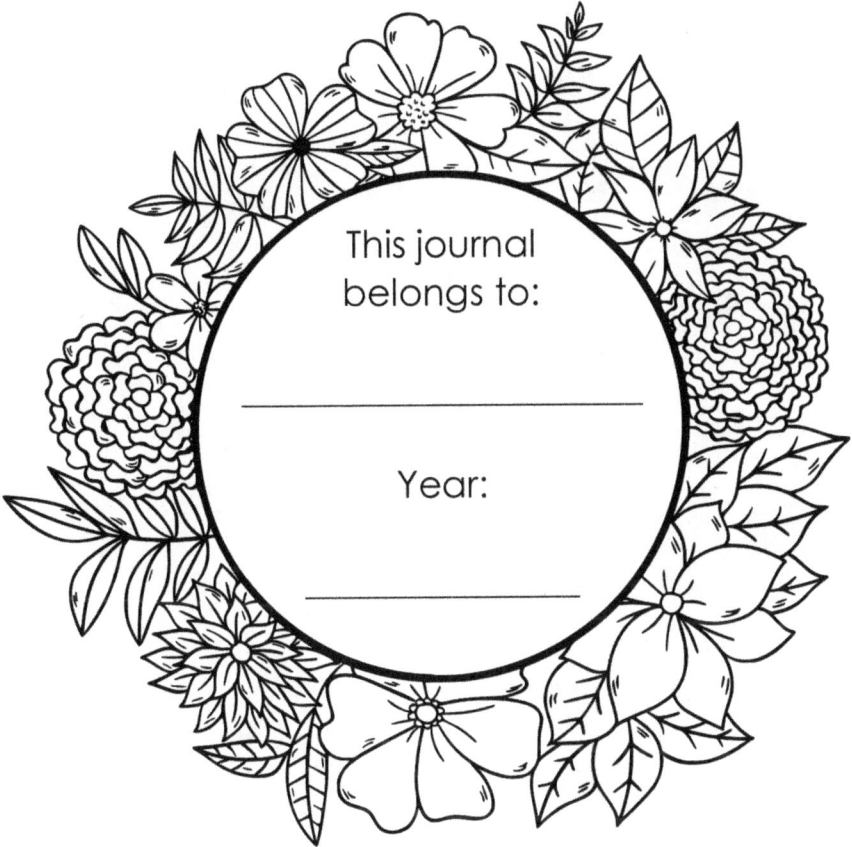

This journal
belongs to:

_____

Year:

_____

I created this art journal with the hope that it will help others to see the wonder and beauty in their every day lives. There is always something to be grateful for, and I believe that we can find joy even in the midst of our darkest trials.

- Shaela Kay -

John 16:20

Published by Blue Water Books
Richland, WA

Cover photo © Adobe/daffodilred
Cover design © Blue Water Books

© 2017 Shaela Kay Odd
Visit the author at www.shaelakay.com

For my mother,
with love

Week 1

Birthdays are special times to celebrate your life and the extraordinary person that you are. What is one of your most memorable birthday experiences? How do you usually like to celebrate? What would you like to do for your next birthday?

_____

_____

_____

_____

_____

_____

_____

_____

_____

_____

_____

_____

Week 2

List the things that you accomplished this week. Way to go!

_____

_____

_____

_____

_____

_____

_____

_____

_____

_____

_____

_____

_____

Week 3

Spreading joy can be as simple as smiling at a stranger.
Make a list of ten things you can do, that don't involve a
lot of planning or money, to spread joy to others.

_____

_____

_____

_____

_____

_____

_____

_____

_____

_____

_____

_____

Week 4

What is your favorite time of the day? Why? What do
you like to do during that time?

_____

_____

_____

_____

_____

_____

_____

_____

_____

_____

_____

_____

_____

_____

Week 5

Make a list of the people in your life who inspire you.
In what ways are they an inspiration?

_____

_____

_____

_____

_____

_____

_____

_____

_____

_____

_____

_____

_____

_____

Week 6

Seeking knowledge can be one of the greatest sources of joy in our lives. What are some things you have learned that have brought you happiness? What are some things you would like to learn?

_____

_____

_____

_____

_____

_____

_____

_____

_____

_____

Week 7

Where would you like to be one year from now?
Five years from now? Ten years from now?

_____

_____

_____

_____

_____

_____

_____

_____

_____

_____

_____

_____

_____

_____

Week 8

Reflect on the moments in your life that have brought you
the greatest joy, and list them here.

_____

_____

_____

_____

_____

_____

_____

_____

_____

_____

Week 9

Beauty is abundant in nature. What things or places in the natural world do you find beautiful?

_____

_____

_____

_____

_____

_____

_____

_____

_____

_____

_____

_____

_____

_____

_____

_____

Week 10

Nobody is perfect, but we are all beautiful in our own unique way. List the things that you love about yourself. Try not to think only about your physical appearance.

_____

_____

_____

_____

_____

_____

_____

_____

_____

_____

_____

_____

Week 11

Stepping beyond our fears and insecurities makes us stronger. What are some things you have done that scared you? How did you feel facing your fears?

_____

_____

_____

_____

_____

_____

_____

_____

_____

_____

_____

_____

Week 12

They say that laughter is the best medicine,
so make a list of things that make you laugh.

_____

_____

_____

_____

_____

_____

_____

_____

_____

_____

_____

_____

_____

_____

_____

_____

_____

_____

Week 13

Music is beauty that we hear. List the songs, musicians, or instruments that you love to listen to.

_____

_____

_____

_____

_____

_____

_____

_____

_____

_____

_____

_____

_____

_____

Week 14

Theatrical performances can be beautiful experiences.
Make a list of your favorite plays, tv shows, movies, musicals,
or other performances.

_____

_____

_____

_____

_____

_____

_____

_____

_____

_____

_____

_____

Week 15

Friends are family that you choose. How have your
friends brought joy and beauty to your life?

_____

_____

_____

_____

_____

_____

_____

_____

_____

_____

_____

Week 16

What sorts of things do you like to create?
How do you add beauty to your home or workplace?

_____

_____

_____

_____

_____

_____

_____

_____

_____

_____

_____

_____

_____

_____

Week 17

Think back on the last few days. In what ways did
you bring joy to others?

_____

_____

_____

_____

_____

_____

_____

_____

_____

_____

_____

Week 18

Our world was created in a rainbow of hues.
What colors make you happy? What are some of your
favorite things in those colors?

_____
_____
_____
_____
_____
_____
_____
_____
_____
_____
_____
_____

Week 19

The written word is a powerful thing. Do you enjoy
poetry or novels? List some of your favorites.

_____

_____

_____

_____

_____

_____

_____

_____

_____

_____

_____

_____

_____

_____

Week 20

In what ways does your family bring you joy?

_____

_____

_____

_____

_____

_____

_____

_____

_____

_____

_____

_____

_____

_____

Week 21

What qualities do you find essential in a good friend?
Which of these qualities do you see in yourself?

_____

_____

_____

_____

_____

_____

_____

_____

_____

_____

_____

_____

_____

Week 22

The world has far more beauty than one person can behold in a lifetime. Make a list of the places you would like to visit if you ever have the chance.

_____

_____

_____

_____

_____

_____

_____

_____

_____

_____

_____

_____

_____

_____

_____

Week 23

So many flavors and foods exist in this world. What are some of your favorites? What foods would you like to try?

_____

_____

_____

_____

_____

_____

_____

_____

_____

_____

_____

_____

_____

_____

Week 24

Everyone will face trials in their life, but how we react to them will determine whether they become stumbling blocks or stepping stones. Make a list of the challenges you have overcome and what helped you to conquer them.

_____

_____

_____

_____

_____

_____

_____

_____

_____

_____

_____

_____

Week 25

Who are your favorite fictional characters?
Why do you love or admire them so much?

_____

_____

_____

_____

_____

_____

_____

_____

_____

_____

_____

_____

_____

_____

_____

Week 26

Talents can bless not only our own lives, but the lives of others. What talents do you possess? What talents would you like to develop? How can you share your talents with others?

_____

_____

_____

_____

_____

_____

_____

_____

_____

_____

_____

_____

Week 27

Our world is filled with unique and beautiful creatures.
Which are your favorite animals? What creatures do you
find the most beautiful?

_____

_____

_____

_____

_____

_____

_____

_____

_____

_____

_____

_____

_____

Week 28

History is replete with stories of real life heroes and heroines. Whom do you admire from the annals of history? Why?

_____

_____

_____

_____

_____

_____

_____

_____

_____

_____

_____

_____

_____

_____

Week 29

Make a list of twenty things you are grateful for
right now, this very minute.

_____

_____

_____

_____

_____

_____

_____

_____

_____

_____

_____

_____

_____

_____

_____

_____

Week 30

Goals are dreams with a deadline. What are some of
your dreams? What are some of your goals?

_____

_____

_____

_____

_____

_____

_____

_____

_____

_____

_____

_____

_____

_____

Week 31

Some of the most beautiful things in this world cannot be touched – they are *smelled*. What are some of your favorite smells? What memories are attached to them?

_____

_____

_____

_____

_____

_____

_____

_____

_____

_____

_____

_____

_____

_____

Week 32

We find joy in doing things we love. What are some
of your favorite things to do?

_____

_____

_____

_____

_____

_____

_____

_____

_____

_____

_____

_____

Week 33

Sometimes our mood varies depending on the climate or weather. What is your favorite season and/or weather? What do you like to do when it's like this?

_____

_____

_____

_____

_____

_____

_____

_____

_____

_____

Week 34

Holidays and celebrations are often joyful occasions.
Which ones are your favorites? What traditions are attached
to them that bring you the most joy?

_____

_____

_____

_____

_____

_____

_____

_____

_____

_____

_____

_____

_____

Week 35

Watching others participate in activities that bring them joy helps us to appreciate all that life has to offer. What people or events make you happy to witness? Can you identify why it brings you joy?

_____

_____

_____

_____

_____

_____

_____

_____

_____

_____

_____

_____

_____

Week 36

Make a list of the sounds you hear in your everyday
life that bring you joy.

_____

_____

_____

_____

_____

_____

_____

_____

_____

_____

_____

_____

_____

Week 37

Worry and fear prevent us from feeling joyful. What are some things that have helped you overcome anxieties and embrace happiness?

_____

_____

_____

_____

_____

_____

_____

_____

_____

_____

_____

_____

_____

_____

Week 38

Paintings, sculptures, and other forms of visual art add beauty to the world. Who are your favorite artists? What are some of your favorite pieces of art? Where have you seen art that inspires you?

_____

_____

_____

_____

_____

_____

_____

_____

_____

_____

_____

Week 39

What we put on our bodies can greatly affect our attitude and mood. What are your favorite things to wear?

_____

_____

_____

_____

_____

_____

_____

_____

_____

_____

_____

_____

_____

Week 40

How have you been blessed by the kindness of others this week? This year? In your lifetime?

_____

_____

_____

_____

_____

_____

_____

_____

_____

_____

_____

_____

_____

_____

Week 41

What was your favorite moment of today?
What could have been improved upon?

_____

_____

_____

_____

_____

_____

_____

_____

_____

_____

_____

_____

_____

_____

Week 42

Prayer and meditation are wonderful opportunities to reflect on our experiences. Take a moment now to pray or contemplate the blessings in your life. Afterwards, write down the impressions you felt or the clarity you received.

_____

_____

_____

_____

_____

_____

_____

_____

_____

_____

_____

Week 43

What vocation have you chosen in your life? How does it bring you joy? In what ways does it bless the lives of others?

_____

_____

_____

_____

_____

_____

_____

_____

_____

_____

_____

_____

_____

_____

Week 44

Our perception of beauty changes as we grow. What is something that you now find beautiful that you once did not? What changed your perception?

_____

_____

_____

_____

_____

_____

_____

_____

_____

_____

_____

_____

Week 45

Make a list of your most prized possessions. What has made them personal treasures?

_____

_____

_____

_____

_____

_____

_____

_____

_____

_____

_____

_____

_____

_____

_____

Week 46

Name a goal that you are actively working towards. What did you do this week to bring you closer to your goal? What can you do in the coming week to continue your progress?

_____

_____

_____

_____

_____

_____

_____

_____

_____

_____

_____

_____

_____

_____

_____

Week 47

Milestones help to shape who we are and what we may become. What are some of the most joyful milestones you have achieved? What milestones are you looking forward to reaching?

_____

_____

_____

_____

_____

_____

_____

_____

_____

_____

_____

Week 48

What is the most beautiful place in your world? Why?

_____

_____

_____

_____

_____

_____

_____

_____

_____

_____

_____

_____

_____

Week 49

How do you make yourself physically comfortable?
What brings comfort to you in your surroundings?

_____

_____

_____

_____

_____

_____

_____

_____

_____

_____

_____

_____

_____

Week 50

Think of the coming week. How can you infuse beauty into your current schedule? Make a list of possibilities and select one or two to follow through with.

_____

_____

_____

_____

_____

_____

_____

_____

_____

_____

_____

_____

_____

_____

_____

Week 51

What did you do this past week to add beauty to your schedule? Write about your experience(s) here.

_____

_____

_____

_____

_____

_____

_____

_____

_____

_____

_____

_____

_____

_____

_____

_____

_____

_____

_____

_____

_____

_____

_____

_____

_____

_____

_____

_____

_____

_____

_____

_____

_____

Week 52

What is the greatest compliment you have ever received?
Who gave it to you? How did it make you feel? Write about
the experience here.

_____

_____

_____

_____

_____

_____

_____

_____

_____

_____

_____

_____

_____

_____

_____

_____

_____

_____

_____

_____

_____

_____

_____

_____

_____

_____

_____

_____

_____

This is not the end. It is not even the beginning of the end. But it is, perhaps, the end of the beginning.

- Winston Churchill -

www.ingramcontent.com/pod-product-compliance
Lightning Source LLC
Chambersburg PA
CBHW070048040426
42331CB00034B/2635